A Collection Of 200 Chess Problems

You are holding a reproduction of an original work that is in the public domain in the United States of America, and possibly other countries.You may freely copy and distribute this work as no entity (individual or corporate) has a copyright on the body of the work.This book may contain prior copyright references, and library stamps (as most of these works were scanned from library copies).These have been scanned and retained as part of the historical artifact.

This book may have occasional imperfections such as missing or blurred pages, poor pictures, errant marks, etc. that were either part of the original artifact, or were introduced by the scanning process. We believe this work is culturally important, and despite the imperfections, have elected to bring it back into print as part of our continuing commitment to the preservation of printed works worldwide. We appreciate your understanding of the imperfections in the preservation process, and hope you enjoy this valuable book.

A COLLECTION OF

200

Chess Problems

COMPOSED BY

FRANK HEALEY

DURING THE YEARS
— 1848 to 1904 —

Including positions which gained prizes in the "Era" Tournament,
1856; in the Competitions held by the British Chess
Association at Manchester, 1857; Birmingham,
1858; Bristol, 1861; London, 1872, and
in the London "Chess Monthly"
Tournament, 1886.

SELECTED and ARRANGED

BY

PERCY HEALEY.

1908.

AMATEUR"

HARVARD COLLEGE LIBRARY
BEQUEST OF
JAMES W. HAYWARD

PREFACE.

A VOLUME like the present, consisting of a collection of problems which serves to illustrate a life's work in problem composition extending over a period of more than fifty years, would be incomplete without a few remarks referring to the author of the positions which fill the following pages. To the writer, who has, during the years of a none too industrious novitiate, been at all times more of an observer of than a competitor in the struggle for problem fame, the works of Frank Healey have naturally offered exceptional inducements for examination and study; and although, in general, a certain precedence might readily enough be conceded to other critics, whose positions in the chess world have been deservedly won by their admirable productions, yet, for the occasion which has presented itself, it will be granted that the compiler of this book has had special opportunities for becoming familiar with the composer's methods and views.

It is at all times an interesting proceeding to compare contemporary talent with that of an earlier day, and from an examination of the classical examples to be found in this collection at least one feature will be discovered which is distinctive of the period in which Healey admittedly held first place. The strictly impartial judge will, however, agree that the difference between the two periods is not so marked as some writers have taken pains to lead the casual reader to infer. Indeed, the chess problem as at present known, so far from being the invention of a certain group of composers who have adopted the title of the *Modern School*, really had its birth about half a century ago, and nearly all the points which are regarded by modern experts as contributing towards the merit of a position were fully appreciated by Healey and his contemporaries long before the misleading terms *transition* and *modern school* were invented. To refer, for example, to "economy of force," it will be found that composers of Healey's day possessed a perfectly clear perception of that principle, although they did not consider it necessary to dilate upon the point, and prize problems of recent years are no more economically constructed than were the most worthy examples of Healey and John Brown. But these composers, while really giving birth to a feature which their followers have only given a name to, were true enough artists to refrain from confounding cause with effect. Briefly, their finished productions were models of economy, not by reason of their straining after that effect, but because they possessed the genius of presenting their thought or inspiration in the happiest and truest form.

The principal change which the reader will observe, upon comparing the following problems with those of a more recent date, is in respect of the strategy involved in their solutions. An elegant chess problem may be said to consist of three chief attributes—strategy, originality and construction, and although some modern writers would probably include variety amongst its leading features, the accomplished chess-player (to whom a problem should pre-eminently appeal), would, with little doubt, consider this to be merely a secondary consideration, dependent entirely on the peculiar exigencies which may arise in the course of construction. For nothing could be more strangely opposed to artistic methods than an attempt to embellish a position by the addition of extraneous variations, which, being foreign to the idea which the composer originally set himself to present, only serve to complicate the plot in an illegitimate manner, while they tend to obscure any beauty there may be in the main line of attack. This was perhaps the strongest view held by Frank Healey, and, as is not seldom the case, the one over which some of his critics have misunderstood him the most. He has been termed, presumably on that account, a "thematic" composer, but this curious appellation only signifies that his problems are masterpieces of chess strategy. Grimshaw, Campbell and Bayer were, by the same reasoning, "thematic" too, as are some, including the best of the Bohemian school, to-day.

The same inventive band of problem enthusiasts, who have chosen for themselves the title of the *modern school*, have applied their talents to the coining of modern terms, such as model and mirror mates. Now although the honour of classifying these particular mating positions may be duly accorded to the *modern school*, it must be remembered that the positions themselves were well known, even to the ancients, and the student will, if he cares to take so much pains, find specimens of such in *Alexandre* and certain old manuscripts preserved in the British Museum. These positions, however, bear little nearer relation to chess strategy than does the final position in one of Herr Lasker's masterpieces bear to the strategy which served to bring about his opponent's downfall. How easy is it to imagine a bewildered and unhappy student poring over the instructions of a modern manual, and dreaming, in the days of his apprenticeship, of the time when he may be able to compose a problem on the lines laid down! Such a production may be entirely in accordance with what he has learned and may even be awarded a prize by the readers of a provincial journal, but it will not necessarily be a specimen of artistic chess. But other students, too, will arise, as they have before, future

Campbells and Healeys amongst the workers in the little realm of chess, with perception keener and a more liberal knowledge of the game, artists who will rise above and renounce the narrow limitations prescribed by a section of purists who will have passed away. May they rather learn to replace numerous variations and artificial mating positions by beautiful and subtle ideas, and the natural consequence will be that their problems will only have lost in mechanical neatness what they will have gained in respect of art.

But it is far from the writer's desire to suggest a controversy respecting the comparative merits of problem masters, and it will doubtless be of more interest to that section of chess players which takes a delight in the more imaginative branch of the game to learn a few facts concerning the chess career of the author under notice. On November 19th, in the year 1828, rather more than a stone's throw from the premises in Rathbone Place, W., which afterwards came to be appropriated by Kling and used by him as a chess resort, Frank Healey was born. He was the second son of a somewhat numerous family, and, with his brothers, was educated at a boarding-school in Kelvedon, Essex. There he learned the moves of the game at which, afterwards, he shone with so much distinction, and early taking a delight in solving the few problems which were to be met with in those days, it was naturally not long before he tried his hand at composition. Two-movers were unconsidered trifles and his first effort was a direct mate in three moves, which was published by the chess editor of an unpretentious journal—" The Home Circle." This occurred shortly after Healey had left school, in the days when he and his brothers were accustomed to spend a considerable portion of what was perhaps a rather too leisurely life in a chess divan which they had fitted up in the premises occupied by their parents.

Very soon afterwards he came into contact with the chess lions of the day—Staunton, Anderssen, Lowenthal, Boden, Harrwittz, Kling—all the stars of that brilliant time were his intimates. "When I see your latest problem," said Lowenthal, "I think, at last I have seen your masterpiece; and the conviction remains—until I solve your next!" Kling was a musician by profession, but a chess-player and composer by inclination. He made arrangements to teach Frank Healey music and visited his house for that purpose. But a chess board was in sight, and Kling, seizing the pieces, set up a position. His pupil, with a fervour no less pronounced, solved and criticised the problem, then showed his tutor another. Is there an enthusiast reading these pages who can fail to guess? All thoughts of music had flown for ever, and what were to have been periodical visits for the purpose of tuition were turned into opportunities for chess evenings. Herr Kling was of an excitable temperament; he would snatch a piece out of Healey's hand and offer to fight over the square it ought to occupy. Although excelling as an analyst and a composer of many fine end-games, he never ranked in the highest class as a composer of direct mate positions.

Later on a new generation of players grew up around Healey and his relative position changed. From being regarded as a youthful genius he came to be considered the authority on all matters relating to problems. Steinitz, Zukertort, Mason and other famous players of the later period, praised not only his problems but his game also. He held his own with Campbell and Steinitz, and it was predicted that he would win great honours as a player. But his love always leaned towards problems, and, being singularly unambitious in all things, he had no ambition whatever as regards prowess across the board.

PREFACE.

Frank Healey was connected in several ways with the literary branch of chess. In the year 1866 he was induced by his friends to issue a collection, and a volume of 200 examples of his early efforts was published by Messrs. Longmans and Co. This book has been out of print for many years, and second-hand copies are sought after by collectors of chess libraries. He was editor of a column in a journal which bore the singular title of "Births, Deaths and Marriages," and, later, contributed regular articles and problems to "The Ladies' Treasury."

As regards tournament honours, he was rarely a competitor after the early years of his career, but it is a fact, as recently stated in the columns of a popular magazine, that on no occasion did his competing problem, or set of problems, fail to gain honours. He was awarded second prize in the famous "Era" tournament (arranged by Lowenthal, 1856), and first prizes in each of the competitions held by the British Chess Association respectively at Manchester, 1857, Birmingham, 1858, and at Bristol, 1861. He was also awarded the special prize for three-movers in the London tournament, 1872, and first prize for two-movers in the London "Chess Monthly" tournament of 1886. Upon the award in connection with the Bristol tournament being published, the chess public was startled by an entirely original and sensational idea in the form of a three-mover. So much has been written in reference to this problem (No. 13 in present collection), that it would be superfluous to remark upon it at length upon this occasion, but it may be of interest to the student of problems to learn the object of the apparently useless white rook on KB3. When the composer conceived the idea of making a rook clear a passage for the queen, the time had almost expired for competing sets to be sent in, and he had, in consequence, but little time to consume over the composition of a finished problem. The task, however, appeared to be satisfactorily accomplished with a white pawn where the rook stands, and the position was sent to Kling for examination as regards cooks, etc. This chess enthusiast was on the point of returning the position to the author, when he discovered a second solution, and only at the last moment was the problem corrected by Healey by the substitution of a rook for the pawn on the square previously referred to.

Critical comment upon the examples which have been chosen for this collection is unnecessary; eulogy, it is felt, would be out of place. But the task of preparing a permanent souvenir of a composer whose name is recognized wherever the game is played and problem composing indulged in, has, besides proving a fascinating occupation, been regarded also as something of a duty; and in the hope that this volume will be welcomed as an addition to the chess library lies the compiler's only expectation of reward.

Frank Healey died on February 17th, 1906, at sunset.

PERCY HEALEY.

Problems in Two Moves.

PROBLEM 1.

"CHESS MONTHLY" TOURNAMENT, 1886.

Motto: "The old and the new."

PROBLEM 2.

BLACK

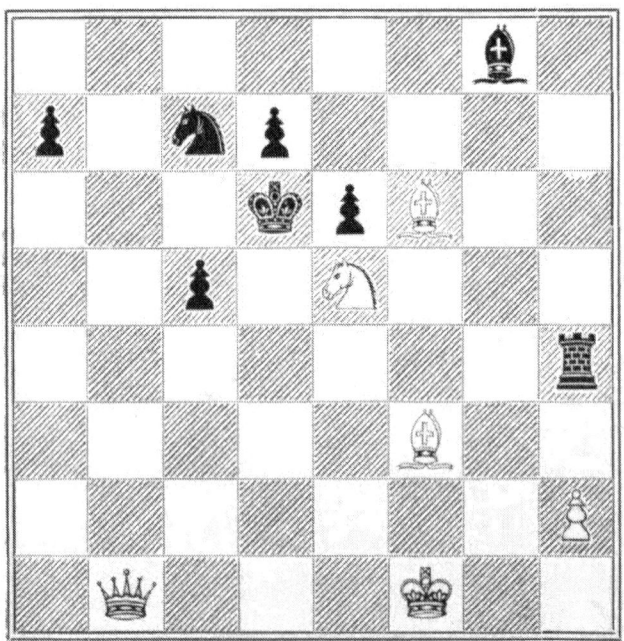

WHITE

White to play and mate in two moves

PROBLEM 3.

BLACK

WHITE

White to play and mate in two moves.

PROBLEM 4.

BLACK

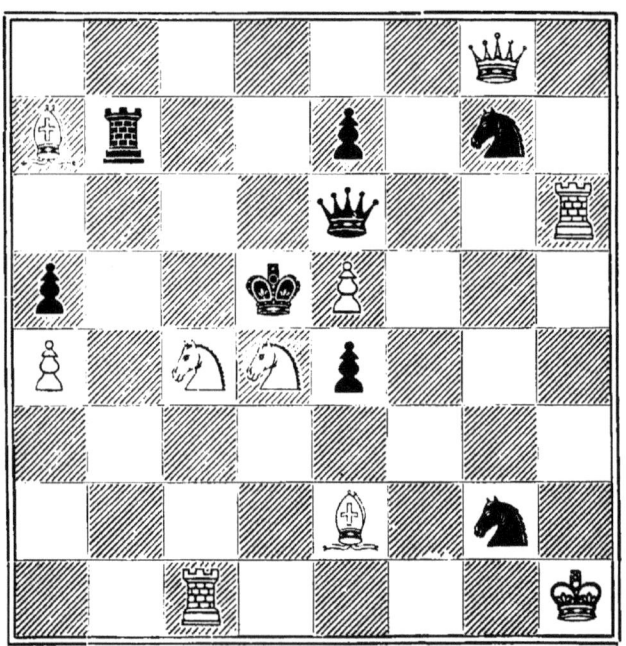

WHITE

White to play and mate in two moves.

PROBLEM 5.

BLACK

WHITE

White to play and mate in two moves.

PROBLEM 6.

BLACK

WHITE

White to play and mate in two moves.

PROBLEM 7.

BLACK

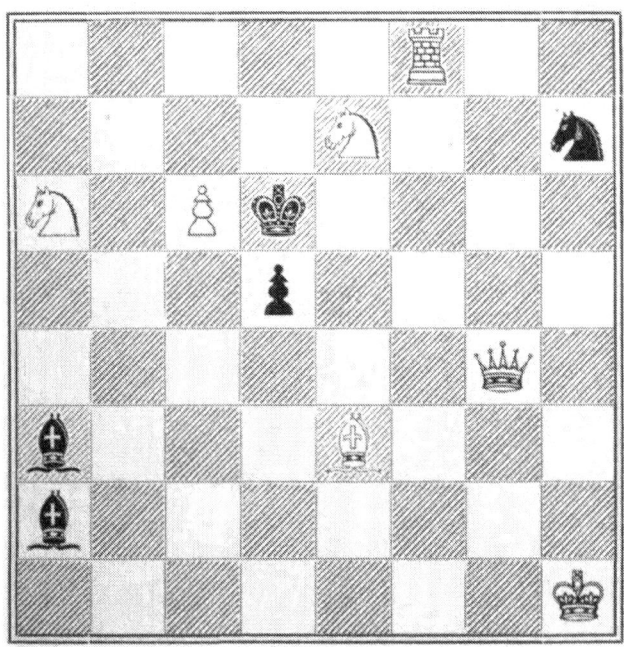

WHITE

White to play and mate in two moves.

PROBLEM 8.

BLACK

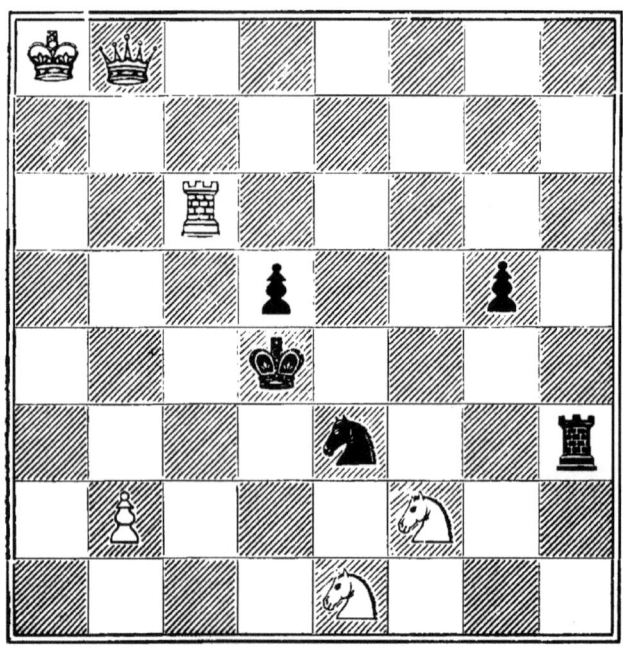

WHITE

White to play and mate in two moves.

PROBLEM 9.

BLACK

WHITE

White to play and mate in two moves.

PROBLEM 10.

BLACK

WHITE

White to play and mate in two moves.

Problems in Three Moves.

PROBLEM 11.

"Era" Tournament, 1856.

Motto: "Palmam qui meruit ferat."

BLACK

WHITE

White to play and mate in three moves.

PROBLEM 12.

BRITISH CHESS ASSOCIATION, MANCHESTER, 1857.

Motto: "*Ludimus effigiem belli.*"

BLACK

WHITE

White to play and mate in three moves.

PROBLEM 13.

British Chess Association, Bristol, 1861.

Motto: "The Climax."

BLACK

WHITE

White to play and mate in three moves.

PROBLEM 14.

BRITISH CHESS ASSOCIATION, BRISTOL, 1861.

BLACK

WHITE

White to play and mate in three moves.

PROBLEM 15.

LONDON TOURNAMENT, 1872.

BLACK

WHITE

White to play and mate in three moves.

PROBLEM 16.

BLACK

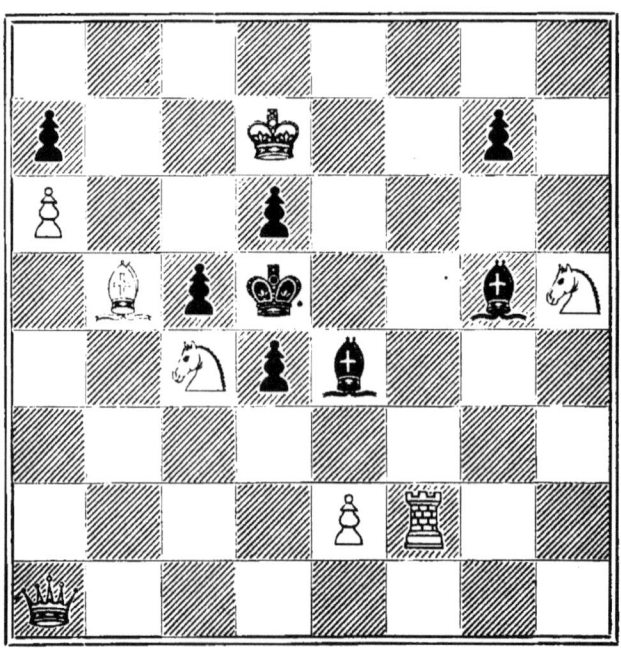

WHITE

White to play and mate in three moves.

PROBLEM 17.

BLACK

WHITE

White to play and mate in three moves.

PROBLEM 18.

BLACK

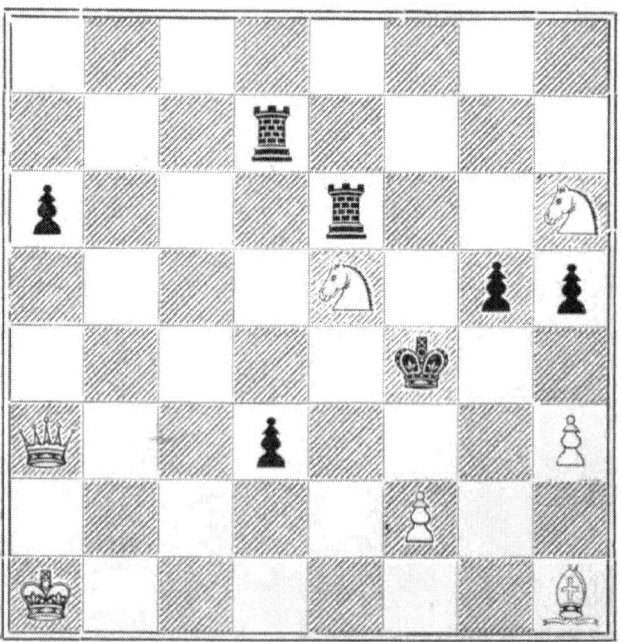

WHITE

White to play and mate in three moves.

PROBLEM 19.

BLACK

WHITE

White to play and mate in three moves.

PROBLEM 20.

BLACK

WHITE

White to play and mate in three moves.

PROBLEM 21.

BLACK

WHITE

White to play and mate in three moves.

PROBLEM 22.

BLACK

WHITE

White to play and mate in three moves.

PROBLEM 23.

BLACK

WHITE

White to play and mate in three moves.

PROBLEM 24.

BLACK

WHITE

White to play and mate in three moves.

PROBLEM 25.

BLACK

WHITE

White to play and mate in three moves.

PROBLEM 26.

BLACK

WHITE

White to play and mate in three moves.

PROBLEM 27.

BLACK

WHITE

White to play and mate in three moves.

PROBLEM 28.

BLACK

WHITE

White to play and mate in three moves.

PROBLEM 29.

BLACK

WHITE

White to play and mate in three moves.

PROBLEM 30.

White to play and mate in three moves.

PROBLEM 31.

White to play and mate in three moves.

PROBLEM 32.

BLACK

WHITE

White to play and mate in three moves.

PROBLEM 33.

BLACK.

WHITE.

White to play and mate in three moves.

PROBLEM 34.

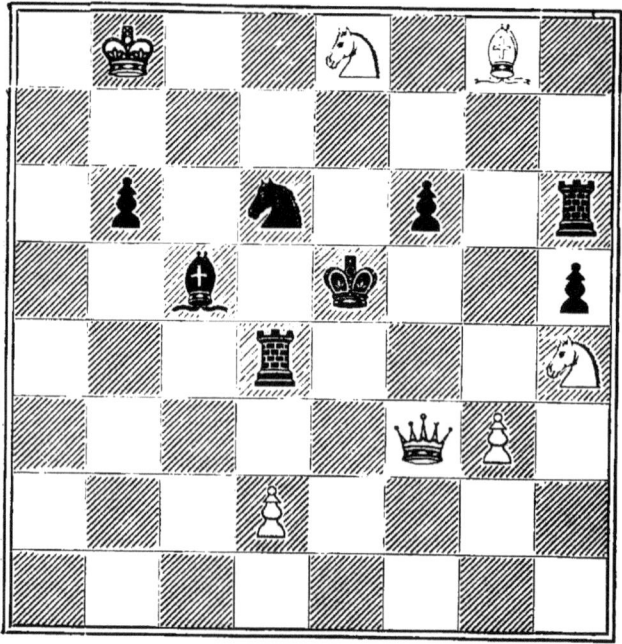

White to play and mate in three moves.

PROBLEM 35.

BLACK

WHITE

White to play and mate in three moves.

PROBLEM 36.

BLACK

WHITE

White to play and mate in three moves.

PROBLEM 37.

BLACK

WHITE

White to play and mate in three moves.

PROBLEM 38.

BLACK

WHITE

White to play and mate in three moves.

PROBLEM 39.

BLACK

WHITE

White to play and mate in three moves.

PROBLEM 40.

BLACK

WHITE

White to play and mate in three moves.

PROBLEM 41.

BLACK

WHITE

White to play and mate in three moves.

PROBLEM 42.

BLACK

WHITE

White to play and mate in three moves.

PROBLEM 43.

BLACK

WHITE

White to play and mate in three moves.

PROBLEM 44.

BLACK

WHITE

White to play and mate in three moves.

PROBLEM 45.

BLACK

WHITE

White to play and mate in three moves.

PROBLEM 46.

BLACK

WHITE

White to play and mate in three moves.

PROBLEM 47.

BLACK

WHITE

White to play and mate in three moves.

PROBLEM 48.

BLACK

WHITE

White to play and mate in three moves.

PROBLEM 49.

BLACK

WHITE

White to play and mate in three moves.

PROBLEM 50.

BLACK

WHITE

White to play and mate in three moves.

PROBLEM 51.

BLACK

WHITE

White to play and mate in three moves.

PROBLEM 52.

BLACK

WHITE

White to play and mate in three moves.

PROBLEM 53.

BLACK

WHITE

White to play and mate in three moves.

PROBLEM 54.

BLACK

WHITE

White to play and mate in three moves.

PROBLEM 55.

BLACK

WHITE

White to play and mate in three moves.

PROBLEM 56.

BLACK

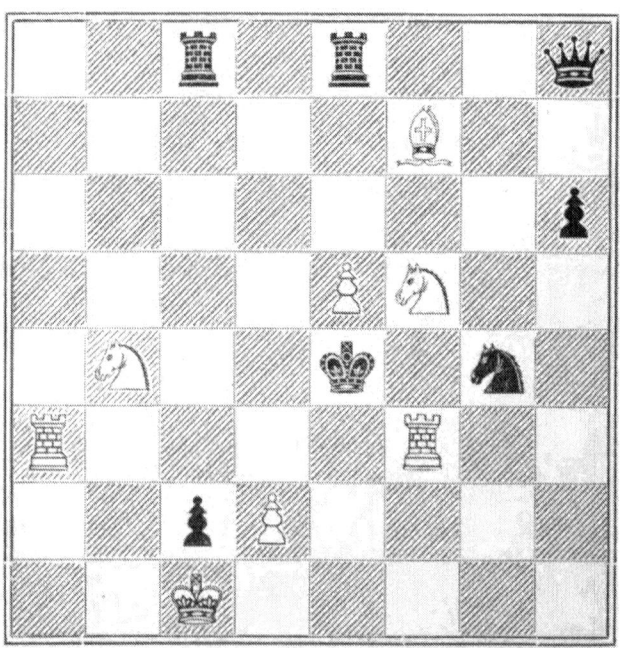

WHITE

White to play and mate in three moves.

PROBLEM 57.

BLACK

WHITE

White to play and mate in three moves.

PROBLEM 58.

BLACK

WHITE

White to play and mate in three moves.

PROBLEM 59.

BLACK

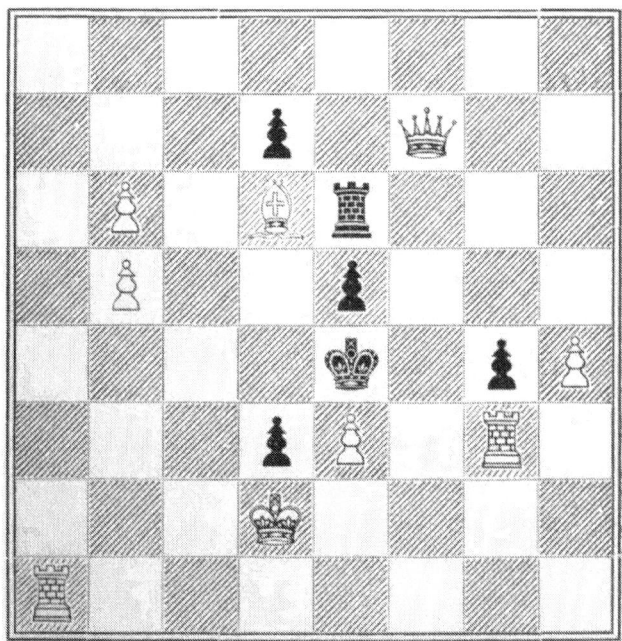

WHITE

White to play and mate in three moves.

PROBLEM 60.

BLACK

WHITE

White to play and mate in three moves.

PROBLEM 61.

BLACK

WHITE

White to play and mate in three moves.

PROBLEM 62.

BLACK

WHITE

White to play and mate in three moves.

PROBLEM 63.

BLACK

WHITE

White to play and mate in three moves.

PROBLEM 64.

White to play and mate in three moves.

PROBLEM 65.

BLACK

WHITE

White to play and mate in three moves.

PROBLEM 66.

BLACK

WHITE

White to play and mate in three moves.

PROBLEM 67.

BLACK

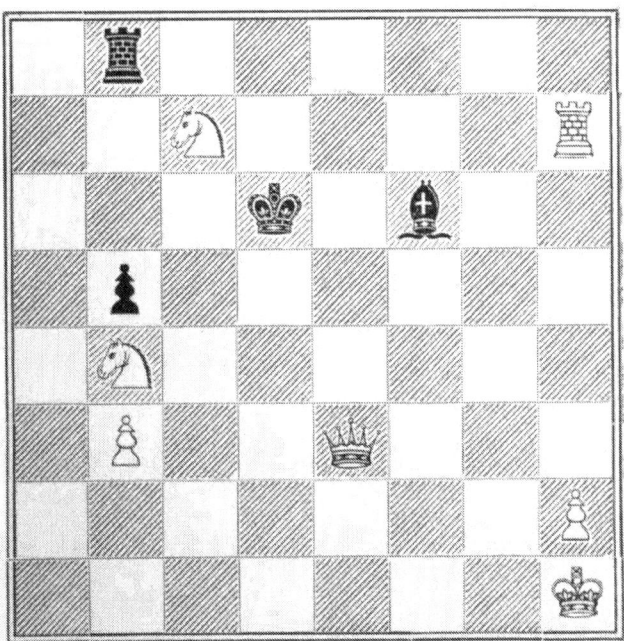

WHITE

White to play and mate in three moves.

PROBLEM 68.

BLACK

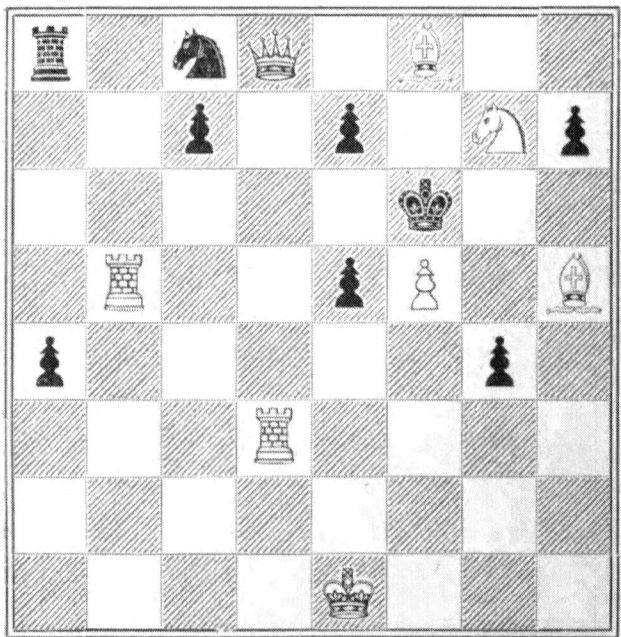

WHITE

White to play and mate in three moves.

PROBLEM 69.

BLACK

WHITE

White to play and mate in three moves.

PROBLEM 70.

White to play and mate in three moves.

PROBLEM 71.

BLACK

WHITE

White to play and mate in three moves.

PROBLEM 72.

BLACK

WHITE

White to play and mate in three moves.

PROBLEM 73.

White to play and mate in three moves.

PROBLEM 74.

White to play and mate in three moves.

PROBLEM 75.

BLACK

WHITE

White to play and mate in three moves.

PROBLEM 76.

BLACK

WHITE

White to play and mate in three moves.

PROBLEM 77.

BLACK

WHITE

White to play and mate in three moves.

PROBLEM 78.

BLACK

WHITE

White to play and mate in three moves.

PROBLEM 79.

BLACK

WHITE

White to play and mate in three moves.

PROBLEM 80.

BLACK

WHITE

White to play and mate in three moves.

PROBLEM 81.

BLACK

WHITE

White to play and mate in three moves.

PROBLEM 82.

BLACK

WHITE

White to play and mate in three moves.

PROBLEM 83.

BLACK

WHITE

White to play and mate in three moves.

PROBLEM 84.

BLACK

WHITE

White to play and mate in three moves.

PROBLEM 85.

BLACK

WHITE

White to play and mate in three moves.

PROBLEM 86.

BLACK

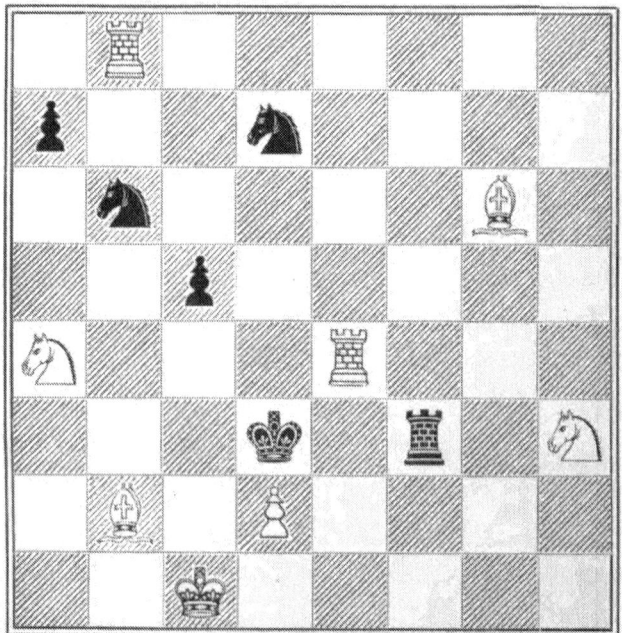

WHITE

White to play and mate in three moves.

PROBLEM 87.

BLACK

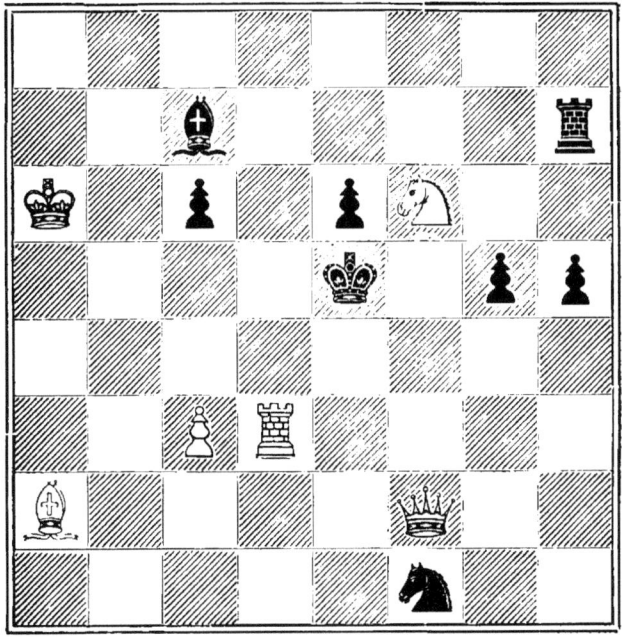

WHITE

White to play and mate in three moves.

PROBLEM 88.

BLACK

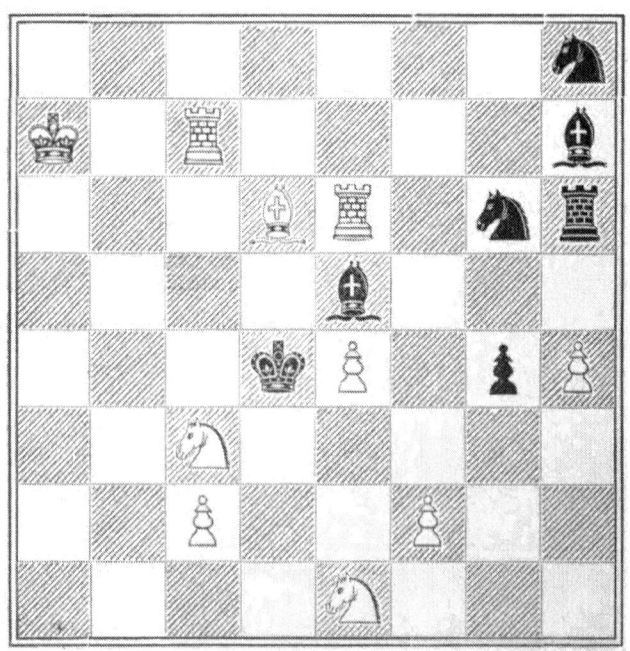

WHITE

White to play and mate in three moves.

PROBLEM 89.

BLACK

WHITE

White to play and mate in three moves.

PROBLEM 90.

White to play and mate in three moves.

PROBLEM 91.

BLACK

WHITE

White to play and mate in three moves.

PROBLEM 92.

BLACK

WHITE

White to play and mate in three moves.

PROBLEM 93.

BLACK

WHITE

White to play and mate in three moves.

PROBLEM 94.

BLACK

WHITE

White to play and mate in three moves.

PROBLEM 95.

BLACK

WHITE

White to play and mate in three moves.

PROBLEM 96.

BLACK

WHITE

White to play and mate in three moves.

PROBLEM 97.

BLACK

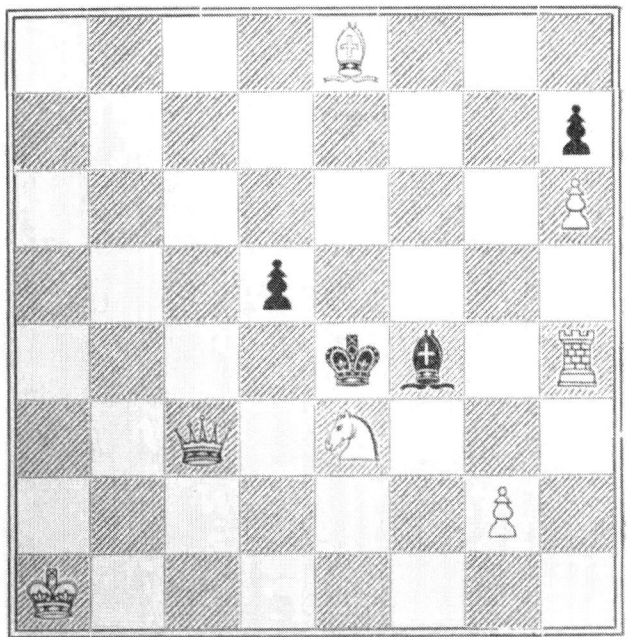

WHITE

White to play and mate in three moves.

PROBLEM 98.

BLACK

WHITE

White to play and mate in three moves.

PROBLEM 99.

BLACK

WHITE

White to play and mate in three moves.

PROBLEM 100.

BLACK

WHITE

White to play and mate in three moves.

PROBLEM 101.

BLACK

WHITE

White to play and mate in three moves.

PROBLEM 102.

BLACK

WHITE

White to play and mate in three moves.

PROBLEM 103.

BLACK

WHITE

White to play and mate in three moves.

PROBLEM 104.

BLACK

WHITE

White to play and mate in three moves.

PROBLEM 105.

BLACK

WHITE

White to play and mate in three moves.

PROBLEM 106.

BLACK

WHITE

White to play and mate in three moves.

PROBLEM 107.

BLACK

WHITE

White to play and mate in three moves.

PROBLEM 108.

BLACK

WHITE

White to play and mate in three moves.

PROBLEM 109.

BLACK

WHITE

White to play and mate in three moves.

PROBLEM 110.

BLACK

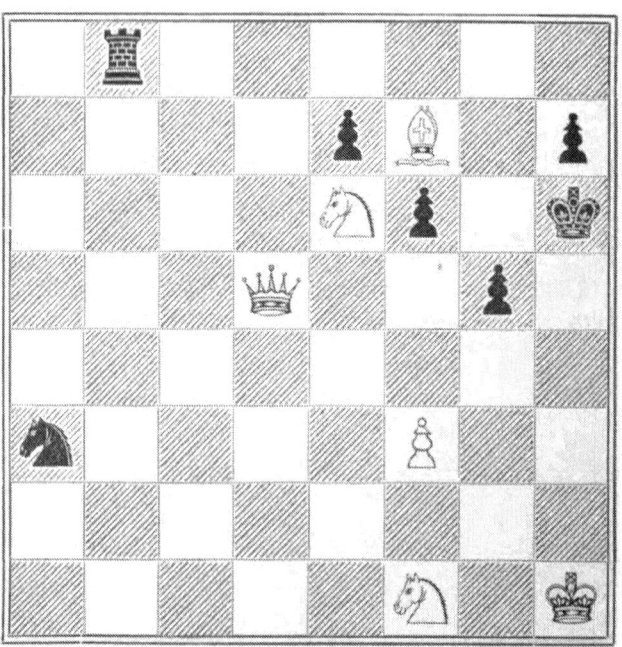

WHITE

White to play and mate in three moves.

PROBLEM 111.

BLACK

WHITE

White to play and mate in three moves.

PROBLEM 112.

BLACK

WHITE

White to play and mate in three moves.

PROBLEM 113.

BLACK

WHITE

White to play and mate in three moves.

PROBLEM 114.

BLACK

WHITE

White to play and mate in three moves.

PROBLEM 115.

BLACK

WHITE

White to play and mate in three moves.

PROBLEM 116.

White to play and mate in three moves.

PROBLEM 117.

BLACK

WHITE

White to play and mate in three moves.

PROBLEM 118.

BLACK

WHITE

White to play and mate in three moves.

PROBLEM 119.

White to play and mate in three moves.

PROBLEM 120.

White to play and mate in three moves.

PROBLEM 121.

BLACK

WHITE

White to play and mate in three moves.

PROBLEM 122.

BLACK

WHITE

White to play and mate in three moves.

PROBLEM 123.

BLACK

WHITE

White to play and mate in three moves.

PROBLEM 124.

BLACK

WHITE

White to play and mate in three moves.

PROBLEM 125.

BLACK

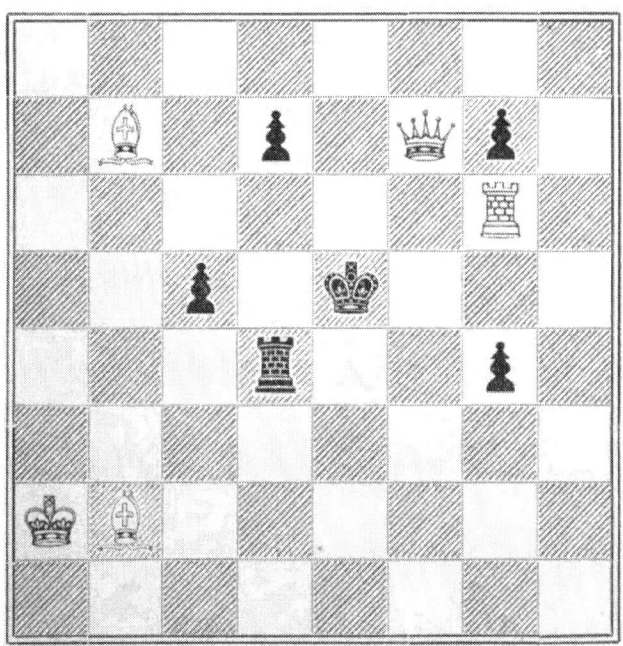

WHITE

White to play and mate in three moves.

PROBLEM 126.

BLACK

WHITE

White to play and mate in three moves.

PROBLEM 127.

BLACK

WHITE

White to play and mate in three moves.

PROBLEM 128.

BLACK

WHITE

White to play and mate in three moves.

PROBLEM 129.

BLACK

WHITE

White to play and mate in three moves.

PROBLEM 130.

White to play and mate in three moves.

PROBLEM 131.

BLACK

WHITE

White to play and mate in three moves.

PROBLEM 132.

BLACK

WHITE

White to play and mate in three moves.

PROBLEM 133.

BLACK

WHITE

White to play and mate in three moves.

PROBLEM 134.

BLACK

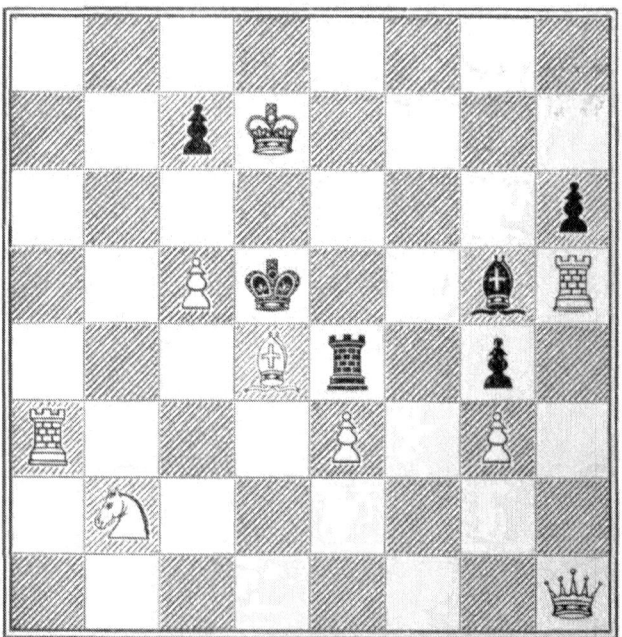

WHITE

White to play and mate in three moves.

PROBLEM 135.

BLACK

WHITE

White to play and mate in three moves.

PROBLEM 136.

BLACK

WHITE

White to play and mate in three moves.

Problems in Four Moves.

PROBLEM 137.

"Era" Tournament, 1856.

BLACK

WHITE

White to play and mate in four moves.

PROBLEM 138.

"Era" Tournament, 1856.

BLACK

WHITE

White to play and mate in four moves.

PROBLEM 139.

"Era" Tournament, 1856.

BLACK

WHITE

White to play and mate in four moves.

PROBLEM 140.

"ERA" TOURNAMENT, 1856.

BLACK

WHITE

White to play and mate in four moves.

PROBLEM 141.

BRITISH CHESS ASSOCIATION, MANCHESTER, 1857.

White to play and mate in four moves.

PROBLEM 142.

BRITISH CHESS ASSOCIATION, BRISTOL, 1861.

BLACK

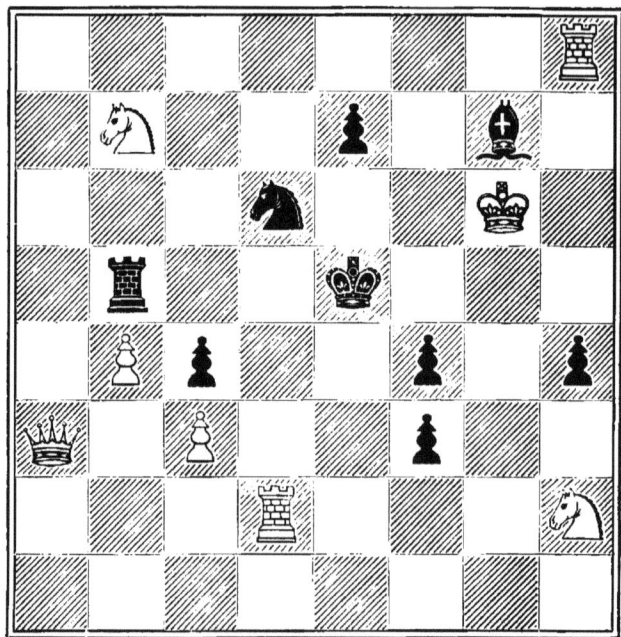

WHITE

White to play and mate in four moves.

PROBLEM 143.

BLACK

WHITE

White to play and mate in four moves.

PROBLEM 144.

BLACK

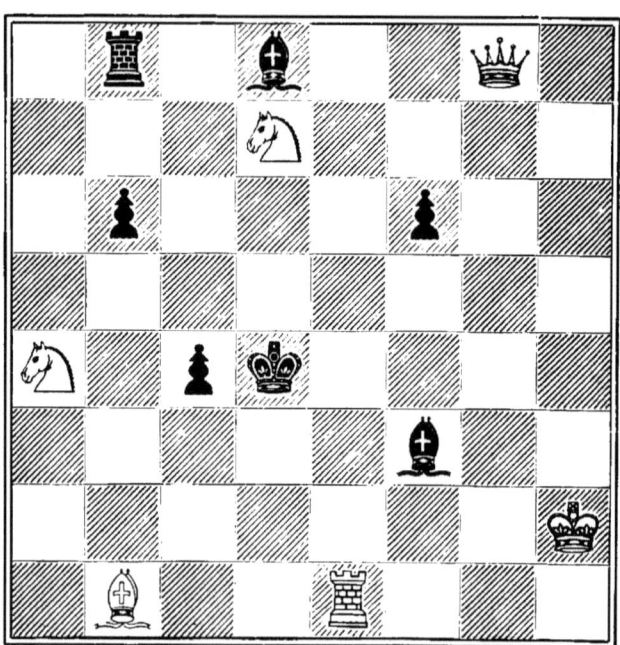

WHITE

White to play and mate in four moves.

PROBLEM 145.

BLACK

WHITE

White to play and mate in four moves.

PROBLEM 146.

BLACK

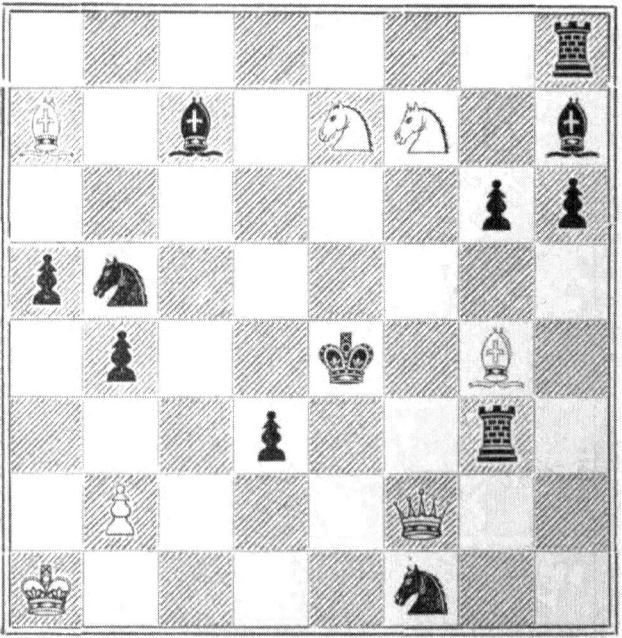

WHITE

White to play and mate in four moves.

PROBLEM 147.

BLACK

WHITE

White to play and mate in four moves.

PROBLEM 148.

BLACK

WHITE

White to play and mate in four moves.

PROBLEM 149.

BLACK

WHITE

White to play and mate in four moves.

PROBLEM 150.

BLACK

WHITE

White to play and mate in four moves.

PROBLEM 151.

BLACK

WHITE

White to play and mate in four moves.

PROBLEM 152.

BLACK

WHITE

White to play and mate in four moves.

PROBLEM 153.

White to play and mate in four moves.

PROBLEM 154.

White to play and mate in four moves.

PROBLEM 155.

BLACK

WHITE

White to play and mate in four moves.

PROBLEM 156.

BLACK

WHITE

White to play and mate in four moves.

PROBLEM 157.

BLACK

WHITE

White to play and mate in four moves.

PROBLEM 158.

BLACK

WHITE

White to play and mate in four moves.

PROBLEM 159.

BLACK

WHITE

White to play and mate in four moves.

PROBLEM 160.

BLACK

WHITE

White to play and mate in four moves.

PROBLEM 161.

BLACK

WHITE

White to play and mate in four moves.

PROBLEM 162.

BLACK

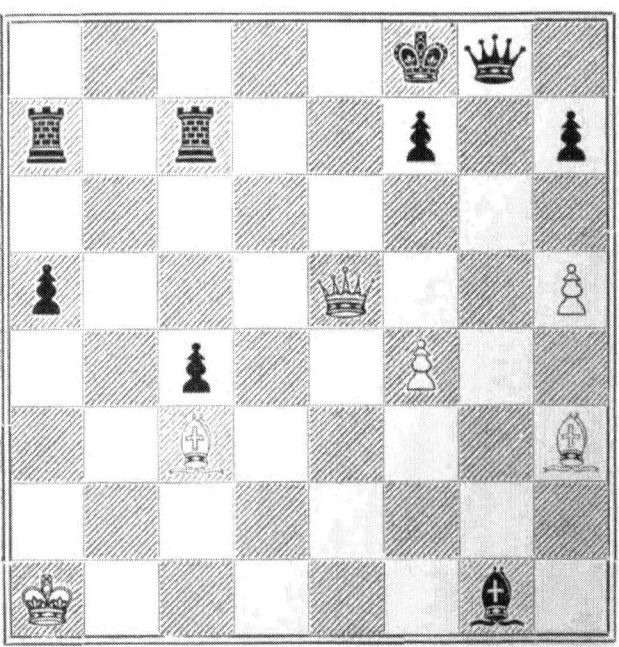

WHITE

White to play and mate in four moves.

PROBLEM 163.

BLACK

WHITE

White to play and mate in four moves.

PROBLEM 164.

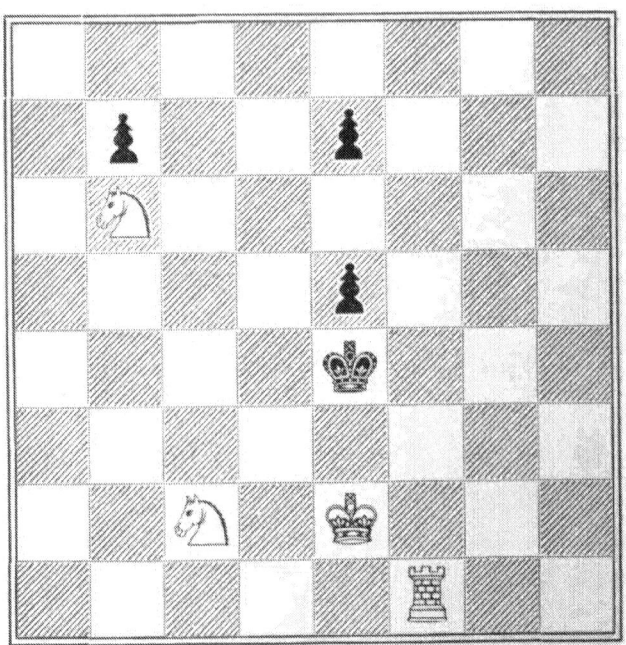

White to play and mate in four moves.

PROBLEM 165.

BLACK

WHITE

White to play and mate in four moves.

PROBLEM 166.

BLACK

WHITE

White to play and mate in four moves.

PROBLEM 167.

BLACK

WHITE

White to play and mate in four moves.

PROBLEM 168.

BLACK

WHITE

White to play and mate in four moves.

PROBLEM 169.

BLACK

WHITE

White to play and mate in four moves.

PROBLEM 170.

White to play and mate in four moves.

PROBLEM 171.

BLACK

WHITE

White to play and mate in four moves.

PROBLEM 172.

BLACK

WHITE

White to play and mate in four moves.

PROBLEM 173.

BLACK

WHITE

White to play and mate in four moves.

PROBLEM 174.

White to play and mate in four moves.

PROBLEM 175.

BLACK

WHITE

White to play and mate in four moves.

PROBLEM 174.

BLACK

WHITE

White to play and mate in four moves.

PROBLEM 175.

BLACK

WHITE

White to play and mate in four moves.

PROBLEM 176.

BLACK

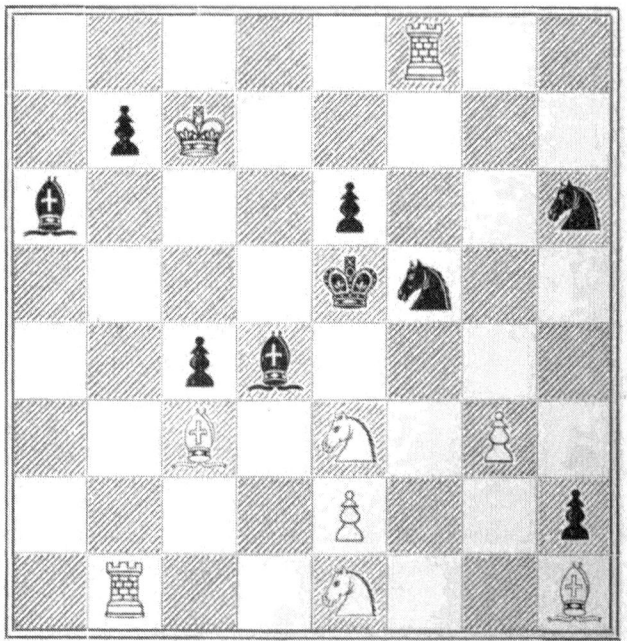

WHITE

White to play and mate in four moves.

PROBLEM 177.

BLACK

WHITE

White to play and mate in four moves.

PROBLEM 178.

White to play and mate in four moves.

PROBLEM 179.

BLACK

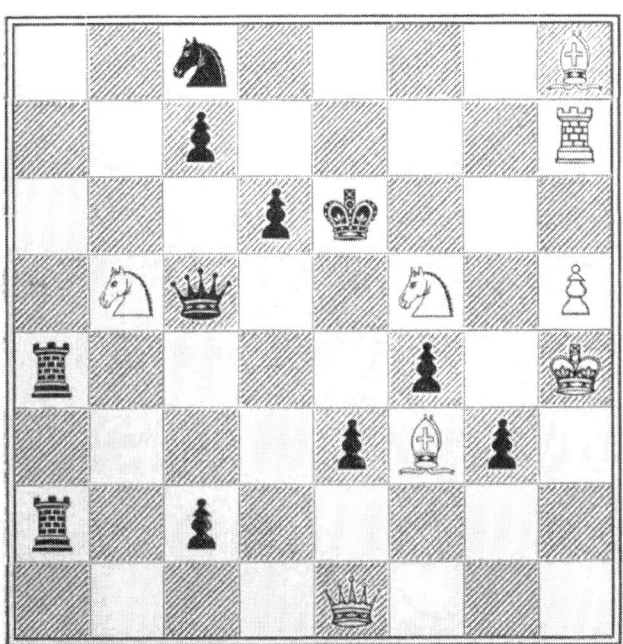

WHITE

White to play and mate in four moves.

PROBLEM 180.

BLACK

WHITE

White to play and mate in four moves.

PROBLEM 181.

BLACK

WHITE

White to play and mate in four moves.

PROBLEM 182.

BLACK

WHITE

White to play and mate in four moves.

Problems in Five Moves.

PROBLEM 183.

BRITISH CHESS ASSOCIATION, BIRMINGHAM, 1858.
MOTTO : *Excelsior*.

BLACK

WHITE

White to play and mate in five moves.

PROBLEM 184.

BRITISH CHESS ASSOCIATION, BRISTOL, 1861.

BLACK

WHITE

White to play and mate in five moves.

PROBLEM 185.

BRITISH CHESS ASSOCIATION, BRISTOL, 1861.

BLACK

WHITE

White to play and mate in five moves.

PROBLEM 186.

BLACK

WHITE

White to play and mate in five moves.

PROBLEM 187.

BLACK

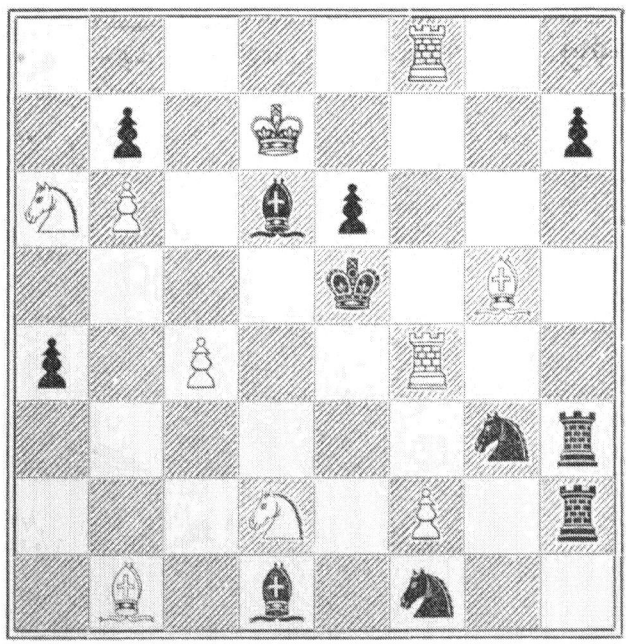

WHITE

White to play and mate in five moves.

PROBLEM 188.

BLACK

WHITE

White to play and mate in five moves.

PROBLEM 189.

BLACK

WHITE

White to play and mate in five moves.

PROBLEM 190.

BLACK

WHITE

White to play and mate in five moves.

PROBLEM 191.

BLACK

WHITE

White to play and mate in five moves.

PROBLEM 192.

White to play and mate in five moves.

PROBLEM 193.

White to play and mate in five moves.

PROBLEM 194.

BLACK

WHITE

White to play and mate in five moves.

PROBLEM 195.

White to play and mate in five moves.

PROBLEM 196.

BLACK

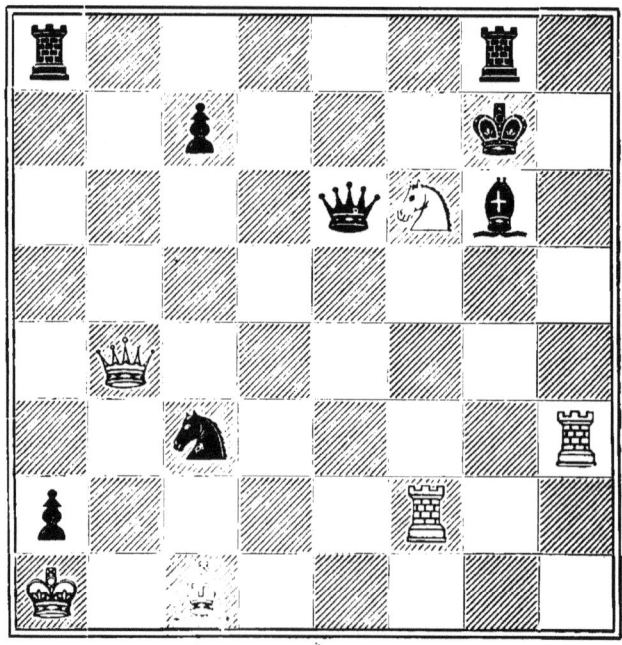

WHITE

White to play and mate in five moves.

PROBLEM 197.

White to play and mate in five moves.

PROBLEM 198.

White to play and mate in five moves.

PROBLEM 199.

BLACK

WHITE

White to play and mate in five moves.

PROBLEM 200.

BLACK

WHITE

White to play and mate in five moves.

SOLUTIONS.

PROBLEMS IN TWO MOVES.

	WHITE			WHITE	
1.	1 R—R6	etc.	6.	1 Q—K7	etc.
2.	1 Q—R7	,,	7.	1 Q—K2	,,
3.	1 Q—Kt	,,	8.	1 Q—R2	,,
4.	1 Kt—B6	,,	9.	1 Q—KB7	,,
5.	1 R—R	,,	10.	1 Q—KR2	,,

PROBLEMS IN THREE MOVES.

	WHITE.	BLACK.	WHITE.	
11.	1 Q—B6	Kt—Kt3	2 R—K5	etc.
12.	1 Q—QB8	R—QR2	2 Q—Kt4	,,
		Kt—B2	2 Q—Kt7	,,
13.	1 R—R	B—K	2 Q—Kt	,,
14.	1 B—K3 dis ch	P—K4	2 Q—Q	,,
		KxKt	2 Q—Kt4 ch	,,
15.	1 Q—KB6	KtxP	2 Q—KB3 ch	,,
		B—Kt6	2 Q—R	,,
		B or Kt—KB4	2 B—Q3 ch	,,

	WHITE	BLACK	WHITE	
16.	1 Q—KR	P—Kt3	2 R—B3	etc.
		BxQ	2 R—B5 ch	,,
17.	1 R—R8	K—K3 or B3	2 Q—R5	,,
		K—B5 or K5	2 Q—Q	,,
18.	1 Q—K7	KxKt	2 Kt—B7 ch	,,
		RxKt (R6)	2 Kt—Kt6 ch	,,
19.	1 Q—QR6	P—K3	2 Kt—K2	,,
20.	1 Kt—B6	BxKt	2 Kt—K7ch	,,
		PxKt	2 Q—R4	,,
		KxKt	2 Q—R6ch	,,
21.	1 R—Kt3	P—Kt4	2 R—R3	,,
		K—K4	2 R—B3 dis ch,,	
22.	1 Q—R6	P—B4	2 KtxBch	,,
		BxQP	2 Q—B8ch	,,
		RxQ	2 B—Kt3ch	,,
23.	1 Q—R7	Kt—K6	2 QxKt(K6)ch	,,
		K moves	2 Kt—Q6	,,
		Kt—Q5	2 Kt—Q6ch	,,
24.	1 Q—QB8	P—B6	2 Q—Q7	,,
		B moves	2 Q—K6ch	,,
25.	1 Kt—Q6	P—Kt6	2 Kt—QB4	,,
		Kt moves	2 Kt—B4ch	,,
26.	1 Kt (R3)—B4	Kt—Kt4	2 Kt—Q2	,,
27.	1 B—B	P—Kt6	2 B—Kt2	,,
28.	1 B—Q3	KxKt	2 B—Kt5 discl,	,,
		P—K8	2 QxBP	,,
		Other	2 QxBP	,,
29.	1 K—Q7	K—K5	2 R—Q5	,,
30.	1 R—Q7	BxR	2 Q—K7ch	,,
		Kt—B5	2 QxKtch	,,
31.	1 R—K6	BxR	2 Q—R6	,,
		RxR	2 Q—Kt2	,,
32.	1 B—B2	K—K6	2 Q—KB6	,,
		K—K4	2 K—B3	,,
33.	1 R—KB6	B—B6	2 K—Kt6	,,

	WHITE	BLACK	WHITE	
34.	1 B—B7	R—K5	2 Q—B5ch	etc.
		B or P moves	2 Q—Q3ch	,,
		KtxKt	2 Q—B5ch	,,
35.	1 R—K8	K—Kt3	2 KtxRP	,,
36.	1 B—Kt4	P—R7	2 Q—R7	,,
		K—B3	2 Q—QB8	,,
37.	1 B—K	B—B4	2 B—B3 ch	,,
		KxR	2 Q—KKt3 ch	,,
		K—B4	2 Q—B7 ch	,,
38.	1 R—B5	RxR	2 B—K4	,,
		R—K5	2 R—B7	,,
39.	1 Q—B8	B—K4	2 R—K8	,,
		K—K5	2 R—K8 ch	,,
40.	1 B—K4	BxB	2 B—K3 ch	,,
		KxKt	2 Q—B5 ch	,,
41.	1 Q—K	K—K3	2 Kt—B4 ch	,,
		Q—K8 or QB8	2 ,,	,,
42.	1 B—K8	K—Q5	2 B—B7	,,
		P—Q5	2 B—R4	,,
43.	1 Q—Q	K—Q3 or R moves	2 Q—Q4	,,
44.	1 R—B7	B—B5	2 Kt—Kt8	,,
		B—Q7, Kt7, or BxP	2 RxKt ch	,,
		B—K6	2 Kt—Kt3	,,
45.	1 K—Kt6	P—Kt5	2 Q—B8	,,
46.	1 B—K4	B—K7	2 Q—Kt4	,,
		P—K4	2 Q—Kt8	,,
		K—B5	2 QxB ch	,,
47.	1 Q—B8	BxKt	2 Kt—B4	,,
48.	1 P—Kt4	B—KB2	2 KtxRP	,,
		B—K3	2 KtxQB	,,
		B—KR2	2 Kt—K6 ch	,,
		R—Kt4	2 PxP	,,
49.	1 B—R8	P—Kt4	2 BxR	,,

	WHITE	BLACK	WHITE	
50.	1 Kt—B6	PxKt	2 QxB ch	etc.
		KxKt	2 B—B8 ch	,,
		B—Kt7 or K6	2 Kt(K6)—Q4	
		RxKt	2 Q—Q5 ch [ch	
		R—Kt4 or R4	2 B—B8	etc.
		R—K4	2 Kt—Q4 ch	,,
		P—B6	2 Kt(K6)Q4 ch	,,
51.	1 B—KR8	P—Q3	2 R—Kt7	,,
52.	1 QxBP	K—K4	2 Q—B6	,,
		Other	2 QxRch	,,
53.	1 Kt—R8	K—K4	2 BxPch	,,
		P or Kt moves	2 Q—R7ch	,,
54.	1 B—QR4	B—B7	2 P—K4ch	,,
		K or P moves	2 BxB	,,
		Kt—B4	2 BxB	,,
55.	1 R—K5	R—KB	2 Q—R	,,
56.	1 Kt—Q3	KxR	2 B—Q5ch	,,
		QxP	2 Kt—B2ch	,,
		R—B6 or K3	2 R—B4ch	,,
57.	1 Kt—R7	B—Q7 or B8	2 Q—B8	,,
58.	1 Kt—QB7	R—QR or RxP	2 Kt—QKt5ch	,,
		R—KB8	2 RxBch	,,
		P—Kt6	2 R—R4ch	,,
		B—B5 or K5	2 Q—Q2ch	.,
59.	1 R—Q	K—Q4	2 KxP	,,
		R—B3	2 Q—B4ch	,,
		R—Kt3	2 Q—B4ch	,,
60.	1 Kt—K7	P—Kt5	2 R—QB6	,,
61.	1 R—QB	B—Q6	2 Q—B4ch	,,
		BxP	2 R—K	,,
		B elsewhere	2 RxB	,,
62.	1 R—K4	QxP	2 B—K6ch	,,
		Kt—B4	2 B—Kt2	,,
63.	1 B—QB5	PxB	2 Q—R4	,,

	WHITE	BLACK	WHITE	
64.	1 Kt—Kt4	Kt moves	2 Kt—B6ch	etc.
		B moves	2 Q—Kt7ch	,,
65.	1 B—Kt5	B—KB5	2 Kt—KKt3	,,
		B—R2	2 Q—Qch	,,
		P—B5	2 Kt—B6	,,
		RxB	2 Q—Q3ch	,,
66.	1 B—B4	P—Kt6	2 K—R5	,,
67.	1 P—R4	B—K4	2 Kt—K8 ch	,,
68.	1 R—KR3	P—B4	2 R—Kt6 ch	,,
		P—K5	2 Q—Q4 ch	,,
		other	2 Q—Q2	,,
69.	1 K—Kt7	Kt—K5	2 Kt—B8	,,
70.	1 Q—B4	any	2 Q—Kt8	,,
71.	1 Q—Kt2	KtxQ	2 Kt—Q6 ch	,,
		P—Q5	2 Q—KB2	,,
72.	1 Kt—B2	KtxKt	2 R—Q	,,
73.	1 B—R7	K—B6	2 Q—KKt6	,,
		B—KB5	2 Q—KKt6	,,
		B—KB3	2 Q—Q6 ch	,,
		K—Q4	2 Kt—K3 ch	,,
74.	1 Q—Kt	Kt—B2 ch	2 RxKtch	,,
		other	2 Kt—R7 ch	,,
75.	1 R—Kt4	PxR	2 Q—K4 ch	,,
76.	1 Q—KB	Kt—Q or QxQ	2 Kt—Kt6 ch	,,
		Kt—B4	2 Kt—B6 ch	,,
77.	1 Kt—R3	BxKt	2 Kt—B4	,,
		PxKt	2 Kt—KB4 ch	,,
78.	1 Kt—KB6	P—K5	2 R—R7	,,
79.	1 Kt—B4	KxB	2 K—K3	,,
		P—Q4	2 R—K6	,,
80.	1 Q—KB	KxP	2 Q—QR6 ch	,,
		K—K4	2 B—Q4 ch	,,
		Kt or P moves	2 Q—Kt5	,,
81.	1 Kt—K7	R—Kt	2 Kt—R8	,,

	WHITE	BLACK	WHITE	
82.	1 Q—Kt7	P—B6	2 Kt—Kt4 ch	etc.
		K—Q5	2 Kt—B3 dis ch	,,
		RxB	2 Kt—Kt4 ch	,,
83.	1 K—K	P—B6	2 Kt—R2	,,
84.	1 Q—B6	Q—Q6	2 Kt—Kt6 ch	,,
		Q—B5	2 Q—K8ch	,,
		Q—R3	2 Kt—Q7ch	,,
		B—B2	2 Q—B3ch	,,
		QBxP	2 B—B6ch	,,
85.	1 B—B4	PxP	2 Kt—K6	,,
		PxB	2 K—B3	,,
86.	1 R—KB8	RxR	2 B—B6	,,
		RxKt	2 R(B8)—B4	,,
87.	1 R—Q6	KxR	2 Q—QB5ch	,,
88.	1 Kt—Q5	KxP	2 Kt—K3	,,
		Kt—B2	2 Kt—B6	,,
		Kt—B5	2 P—QB3ch	,,
89.	1 Kt—Kt4	R—R6	2 Q—K8	,,
		KxKt	2 Q—KB7	,,
		Q—Kt8	2 Q—KR7ch	,,
		Q—B6	2 Q—B6ch	,,
90.	1 Q—QR4	K—B3	2 Q—R8	,,
91.	1 Kt—Kt2	K—B4	2 Q—Q7ch	,,
		Kt—B2	2 Kt—Q8ch	,,
		P—B4	2 BxRch	,,
92.	1 Kt—B7	KtxKt	2 Q—B3	,,
		Kt—B6	2 Kt—Kt5	,,
93.	1 B—B8	K—B3	2 Q—K6	,,
		B moves	2 Q—K4ch	,,
94.	1 RxP	P—Q4	2 Q—K4ch	,,
		KtxKt	2 Q—K4ch	,,
		PxR	2 Kt—QB5	,,
95.	1 B—R3	KtxR	2 Kt—KR5	,,
		Kt—B6	2 R—Q4ch	,,

	WHITE	BLACK	WHITE	
96.	1 R—Kt	B—Kt7	2 R—QB	etc.
		Other	2 BxKtch	,,
97.	1 B—Kt5	P—Q5	2 Q—Kt4	,,
98.	1 B—Q6	BxB	2 Q—Kt6	,,
		B—Kt2	2 Q—B2	,,
		B—R3 or Kt moves	2 Q—B ch	,,
		R—Kt3	2 Q—B ch	,,
		K—Q6	2 Q—Kt6 ch	,,
99.	1 R—B5	KxR	2 Kt—KB5	,,
100.	1 R—R5	Kt or PxR	2 Q—QR	,,
		Kt—Q3 or P—K4	2 Kt—Q2 ch	,,
101.	1 R—Q4	Kt(R8)—B7	2 B—Q2 ch	,,
102.	1 B—Kt3	P—B5	2 K—B6	,,
		K—Q4	2 Q—Q8	,,
103.	1 Kt—KB5	B—KB5	2 R—K5	,,
104.	1 B—Kt7	KtxB	2 R—K ch	,,
		R—Q	2 R—K ch	,,
105.	1 Kt—K6	B—B3 or KB3	2 Q—Q4 ch	,,
		Kt—B5	2 Q—QB5 ch	,,
		P—B4	2 Q—KKt7 ch	,,
106.	1 R—QKt2	PxR or B—QB7	2 Kt—B2 ch	,,
		K—K5	2 R—K2 ch	,,
107.	1 B—R	B—R4	2 Q—Q7	,,
108.	1 Kt—K5	Kt—B or Kt—Kt6	2 Q—Q3	,,
		BxB	2 Q—K2	,,
109.	1 Kt—B2	RxKt	2 R—Q2 ch	,,
		BxP or B—Kt3	2 Q—Kt5 ch	,,
110.	1 Q—R8	RxQ	2 Kt—K3	,,
111.	1 Q—R7	QxR	2 KtxKP ch	,,
		QxKt	2 QxQ	,,
112.	1 Kt—Kt4	R—K7	2 Kt—QR6	,,
113.	1 Q—KR8	KxKt	2 Q—R2 ch	,,
		Other	2 KtxPch	,,

	WHITE	BLACK	WHITE	
114.	1 Kt—KKt6	BxKt	2 Q—QR2	etc.
		QxR	2 Q—KB5 ch	,,
		QxB or Q—Q5	2 Kt—B8ch	,,
115.	1 QxP	B—B3	2 Kt—QKt6	,,
		B—Q4	2 Q—Q6	,,
116.	1 K—K	P—B6	2 Kt—R2	,,
117.	1 Kt—B8	R—Q3	2 Q—Q7	,,
		R—R3	2 Q—Kt8	,,
118.	1 Q—K6	RxQ	2 P—Q4ch	,,
119.	1 R—Kt8	K moves	2 Q—B6ch	,,
		Other	2 Q—Kt5ch	,,
120.	1 Q—Kt4	BxP	2 Q—K6	,,
		PxKt or K moves	2 QxP	,,
121.	1 R—Kt4	P—R7	2 Q—K3 ch	,,
		K—Q6	2 K—Q5	,,
122.	1 Q—Kt6	QxQ	2 R—Q6	,,
		K—Q4	2 QxKt ch	,,
123.	1 Kt—K3	Kt—Kt3	2 B—QB3	,,
124.	1 Kt—Q4	Kt—Kt5	2 R—K3 ch	,,
		P—B5	2 RxP	,,
125.	1 B—Q5	P—B5	2 Q—B8	,,
		P—Kt6	2 Q—KB3	,,
126.	1 B—R5	Kt moves	2 Q—KB5 ch	,,
		K moves	2 Q—K6 ch	,,
127.	1 Kt—K8	B—K5	2 Kt—QB7	,,
128.	1 R—Kt3	BxR	2 Q—Kt6 ch	,,
		Kt(K) moves	2 Kt—B6 ch	,,
129.	1 R—K7	K—Q4	2 R—Q7 ch	,,
130.	1 B—Kt4	KtxB or Kt—B5	2 B—Q5	,,
		Kt—Kt7	2 Kt—B5 ch	,,
131.	1 B—Kt4	B—Q4	2 Q—K6	,,
		Kt—Q4	2 Q—B5	,,

	WHITE	BLACK	WHITE	
132.	1 Kt—K5	KxKt	2 Q—K3 ch	etc.
		Kt—B2 or Kt—Kt3	2 Q—KB4 ch	,,
		Kt—Q3	2 KxKt	,,
		Kt—B6	2 PxKt ch	,,
		P—Q7	2 Q—QB4 ch	,,
133.	1 Q—B8	KxKt	2 B—QKt6 ch	,,
		K—B4 or B5	2 BxQP dis ch	,,
134.	1 R—R7	P—B3	2 K—B8	,,
135.	1 B—K6	R—B ch	2 KxR	,,
136.	1 P—KKt4	R—Q	2 Kt—B5 ch	,,
		RxP	2 RxB ch	,,
		B—QB6	2 QxP ch	,,

PROBLEMS IN FOUR MOVES.

137. 1 R—Q8, B—Kt8 ; 2 R—Kt8, any ; 3 Kt—QB7 ch, etc.
or 1 ... R—Q2 ; 2 RxR ; B—Kt8, 3 R—Kt7, etc.

138. 1 Q—Kt5, PxKt ; 2 P—Q5 ch, K—K4 ; 3 Q—Kt3 ch, etc.
or 1 ... B—Q ; 2 QxB ; R—Kt2 ch, 3 KtxR ch, etc.

139. 1 Kt—K6, PxKt ; 2 B—K5, PxB ; 3 QxBP, etc.

140. 1 Q—Q8, Kt—K3 ; 2 Q—KB6, BxQ ; 3 R—KB5, etc.
or 2 ... B—KB5 ; 3 RxB ch, or K—Q4 ; 3 Kt—K7 ch, etc.
or 1 ... R—B5 ; 2 Kt—QB5 ch, K moves ; 3 Q—KR4, etc.

141. 1 R—K7, RxB ; 2 Kt—K3, BxKt ; 3 Kt—K5, etc.
or 2 ... R—KKt ; R—K4 ch, etc.
or 1 ... P—KB4 ; 2 Kt—K3, BxKt ; 3 Kt—R8, etc.
or 2 ... B—K4 ; 3 RxB, etc.

142. 1 Q—R7, Kt—KB4 ; 2 Kt—KKt4 ch, K—K5 ; 3 Q—R8, etc.
or 1 ... RxKt, 2 KtxPch ; K—K3, 3 Kt—Kt5, etc.
or 1 ... KtxKt, 2 Q—Q4ch ; K moves, 3 Q—Q7ch, etc.
or 1 ... K—K5, 2 KtxKtch ; PxKt, 3 R—K8ch, etc.
or 1 ... B—KB3, 2 KtKKt4ch ; K—K5, 3 R—Q4ch, etc.
or 1 ... R—Q4, 2 Q—B5 ; etc.

143. 1 K—Kt3, K—Q5 ; 2 Q—QB7, K moves ; 3 Q—QB2, etc.
or 2 ... P—K5 ; 3 QxQP, etc.

144. 1 Kt—K5, PxKt ; 2 B—K4, BxB ; 3 Q—Kt4, etc.

145. 1 R—B8ch, KxR ; 2 B—KKt6, B—QB ; 3 R—K6, etc.

146. 1 Kt—Q5, B—K4 ; 2 Q—KB4ch KxKt ; 3 Q—QB4ch, etc.
or 1 ... KxKt ; 2 Q—KB5ch, K moves ; 3 Q—QB4ch, etc.

147. 1 K—Kt, P—Q5 ; 2 Kt—Q5, KxKt ; 3 Q—KB7ch, etc.
or 1 ... K—Q2 ; Q—KB7ch, K—B ; 3 Q—K8ch, etc.

148. 1 Kt—QKt7, R—Kt4 ; 2 Q—QKt8, R—KR8 ; 3 Kt—QB5ch, etc.

149. 1 Q—B6, RxQ ; 2 KtxQch, KxKt ; 3 K—B2, etc.
or 1 ... KxKt ; 2 B—Q2ch, K—K4 ; 3 Q—QB5ch, etc.
or 2 ... K—Kt6 ; 3 Q—KKt2, etc.

150. 1 Q—Kt, Kt—K6 ; 2 Q—KB5ch, KxKt ; 3 Q—QB5ch, etc.
or 1 ... KtxKt ; 2 B—QR3ch, K—B2 ; 3 Q—Kt7ch, etc.

151. 1 R—B4, BxR ; 2 B—Q4ch, PxB ; 3 Kt—K, etc.

152. 1 B—R7, P—R4 ; 2 Q—B3, P—Kt7 ; 3 Q—B8, etc.
or 1 ... P—Kt7 ; 2 Q—Ktch, etc.

153. 1 Kt—Q8, P—K4 ; 2 Kt—B7, Q—Q4 ; 3 R—Q8ch, etc.
or 1 ... Q—B ; 2 R—Q5 dis ch, Q—Q2 ; 3 Kt—K6, etc.

154. 1 Kt(Q7)K5, R—Kt3 ; 2 K—B2, R—B3ch ; 3 K—Kt3, etc.
or 1 ... R—Bch ; 2 K—Kt2, R—B3 ; 3 K—Kt3, etc.

155. 1 Kt—KB6, BxKt ; 2 B—K4, KxB ; 3 Q—QB4ch, etc.

156. 1 Q—R, QxB ; 2 KtxKtPch, PxKt ; 3 Q—QR8, etc.

157. 1 Q—KB7, R—K4 ; 2 Q—B4ch, KxKt ; 3 Q—B4ch, etc.
or 1 ... R—B3 ; 2 Q—K7ch, KxKt ; 3 Kt(R8)Kt6ch, etc.

158. 1 R—QKt7, K—K4 ; 2 B—QB7ch, K—Q5 ; 3 R—Kt2, etc.

159. 1 R—R8, K—Q3 ; 2 B—Kt8ch, K—B4 ; 3 R—R4, etc.
or 1 ... K—K2 ; 2 P—R6, etc.

160. 1 R—K6, RxR ; 2 Q—Kt7, P—K7 ; 3 Q—K4ch, etc.
or 2 ... K—K4 ; 3 Kt—K2ch, etc.

161. 1 Q—R4, B—K3 ; 2 Q—K8, BxR ; 3 KtxBch, etc.
or 2 ... Other ; 3 R—KB5ch, etc.

162. 1 B—Q7, RxB ; 2 Q—Kt8ch, K moves ; 3 B—KB6ch, etc.
or 1 ... B—Q5 ; 2 Q—Q6ch, K moves ; 3 BxBch, etc.

163. 1 Q—QB7, RxP ; 2 Q—R2, QxQ ; 3 RxQ, etc.
or 1 ... K moves ; 2 K—B5, K moves ; 3 Kt—Kt3ch, etc.

164. 1 K—Q2, P—K3 ; 2 K—B, K—Q6 ; 3 R—K, etc.

165. 1 Kt—B4, BxKt ; 2 R—K3 ch, KxR ; 3 R—K5 ch, etc.
or 2 ... K—B5 ; 3 R—Q4 ch, etc.

166. 1 Q—R8, Q—KB2 ; 2 Q—Kt8, QxQ ; 3 R—QB6, etc.
or 1 ... P—Kt5 ; 2 QxQ, P—Kt6 ch ; 3 KxP, etc.

167. 1 R—B4, B—K4 ; 2 Kt—B3, B—Q6 ; 3 R—K4ch, etc.

168. 1 Q—B8, P—K5 ; 2 RxP ch, BxR ; 3 Kt—Kt5 ch, etc.

169. 1 Kt—B4 ch, K—K4 ; 2 R—QR4, P—B4 ; 3 B—Kt4, etc.
or 1 ... K—Q2 ; 2 K—B7, P moves ; 3 Kt—K6, etc.

170. 1 Q—Kt4, K—Q4 ; 2 Kt—K7 ch, K—Q3 ; 3 B—B5 ch, etc.
or 1 ... B moves ; 2 Q—Kt8 ch, B—Q4 ; 3 Q—QB8 ch, etc.

171. 1 Q—R2, KtxR ; 2 QxP, B—Kt5 ; 3 Q—Kt2, etc.

172. 1 Q—B4 B—Kt6 ; 2 B—Kt6, RxB or B—Q3 ; 3 Q—B ch, etc.
or 2 ... K moves ; 3 Q—KB7 ch, etc.

173. 1 R—Q8, RxR ; 2 QxRP, Q—Kt2 ; 3 QxKt ch, etc.

174. 1 R—Kt3, PxR(Kt3) ; 2 R—B5, PxP ; 3 RxR, etc.

175. 1 R—Kt5, Q—K5 ; 2 R—K5, QxR or Kt moves ; 3 QxRP ch, etc.
or 1 ... Q—R3 ; 2 Q—Q5 ch, any ; 3 Q—Q ch, etc.

176. 1 R—Kt4, P—Kt4 ; 2 R—B7, BxB ; 3 Kt—Q3 ch, etc.
or 2 ... B—Kt2 ; 3 RxP ch, etc.

177. 1 Q—K, B—R4 ; 2 K—K7, K—K5 ; 3 Q—Kt4 ch, etc.
or 2 ... B moves ; 3 Q—KR ch, etc.

178. 1 R—K4, Q—Q4 ; 2 Kt—Q6, any ; 3 RxP ch, etc.
or 1 ... Kt—K3 ; 2 Kt—Q6, K—Q4 ; 3 RxP, etc.
or 2 ... Kt—Q ; 3 RxP ch, etc.

179. 1 Q—R5, KxKt ; 2 Kt—B3, K—K3 ; 3 B—Kt4 ch, etc.
or 1 ... other ; 2 Kt—Q4 ch, RxKt ; 3 KtxR ch, etc.

180. 1 K—B, P—Kt5 ; 2 K—Kt2, K—Kt4 ; 3 B—R5, etc.

181. 1 B—QKt, R—K3 ; 2 R—K5, KxR ; 3 B—Kt3 ch, etc.
or 2 ... R—Q3 ; 3 RxR, etc.
or 2 ... RxKt ; 3 RxR(K2), etc.
or 1 ... Kt—KB2 ; 2 R—B4 ch, K moves ; 3 Kt—Kt6 ch, etc.
or 1 ... Kt—Kt3 ; 2 KtxKt, R—K3 ; 3 Kt—R4, etc.

182. 1 R—KB4, B—K5 ; 2 Kt—QB3, B—Q6 ; 3 R—K4 ch, etc.

PROBLEMS IN FIVE MOVES.

183. 1 Q—KB4, B—QKt7 ; 2 Kt—Q6, B—Q5 ; 3 Kt—K4, any ; 4 R—QB5 ch, etc.
or 2 ... R—KB5 ; 3 R—QB5 ch, KxR ; 4 Q—QB4 ch, etc.
or 2 ... R—KR5 ; 3 QxR(K6), R—Q5 ; 4 Kt—K8, etc.
or 3 ... B—Q5 ; 4 Q—KB3 ch, etc.

184. 1 Q—B, B—R4 ; 2 R—Q4, PxR ; 3 Q—KKt5, RxQ ; 4 Kt—KB4, etc.

185. 1 B—KB6, RxB ; 2 Kt—KB2 ch, K—Q5 ; 3 Q—QB, K—K4 ; 4 Q—QB7 ch, etc.
or 3 ... other ; 4 Q—K3 ch, etc.

186. 1 R—KR8, P—Q6 ; 2 R—KR2, P—KB6 ; 3 PxP, P moves ; 4 R—K2, etc.

187. 1 Kt—QB5, BxKt ; 2 R(B8)B5 ch, PxR ; 3 R—Q4, Kt—Kt6 ; 4 P—KB4 ch, etc.

188. 1 B—R3, P moves ; 2 B—Q6 ch, PxB ; 3 K—B6, P moves ; 4 K—B5, etc.

189. 1 R—Kt8, RxB ; 2 Kt—KR6, R—KKt2 ; 3 R—KKt8, any ; 4 Kt—KB7 ch, etc.
or 1 ... P—Q7 ; 2 B—QKt2, R—KB ; 3 Kt—KB6, R—KB2 ; 4 Kt—KR7 ch, etc.

190. 1 B—B ch, R—K6 ; 2 RxP, RxR ; 3 Q—KR8, B—K ; 4 Kt—K6 ch, etc.

191. 1 Kt—QKt3, P moves ; 2 K—Kt7, B—KR3 ch ; 3 K—Kt6, R—Kt3 ch ; 4 KxP, etc.
192. 1 Q—B5, Kt—QB7 ; 2 Q—K7, Q—KB4 ; 3 KtxQP ch, QxKt ; 4 Q—KB6 ch, etc.
  or 2 ... P—KKt5 ; 3 P—KR4, Q—KB4 ; 4 KtxQP ch, etc.
193. 1 RxQBP, RxKt ; 2 Q—KKt8, B—KKt2 ; 3 P—KB8(Kt), RxR ; 4 Q—QB4ch, etc.
  or 1 ... QxKt ; 2 Q—KR, Kt—Q4 ; 3 Q—KKtch, Kt—K6 ; 4 Q—QRch, etc.
  or 1 ... Q—QB2 ; 2 Q—KR, Kt—Q4 ; 3 PxKt, QxR ; 4 Q—K4ch, etc.
  or 3 ... Kt—Q3 ; 4 Q—KKt, etc.
194. 1 Kt—Q6ch, PxKt ; 2 B—QKt7, Kt—QB3 ; 3 B—QR6, KtxP ; 4 R—KB5 dis ch, etc.
  or 2 ... R—KB4 ; 3 RxB, RxR ; 4 B—QR6, etc.
195. 1 R—B6, PxR ; 2 Q—KB3, R—Q5 ; 3 Q—KB6ch, K—K5 ; 4 Q—KB4ch, etc.
196. 1 R—R7ch, BxR ; 2 Kt—KR5ch, K—Kt3 ; 3 Q—KKt4ch, QxQ ; 4 R—KB6ch, etc.
197. 1 B—KB6ch, K—KB4 ; 2 Q—K4ch, KxQ ; 3 Kt—Q6ch, K moves ; 4 P—B4ch, etc.
198. 1 Q—QR2, R—K ; 2 Q—KKt2, BxKt ; 3 KtxKRPch, K—K4 ; 4 Q—KKt3, etc.
  or 2 ... R—KKt ; 3 Kt—K2, PxKt ; 4 Q—KB2ch, etc.
199. 1 R—K7ch, B—K3 ; 2 P—Q4ch, PxP en pass ; 3 R—Q4, KtxR ; 4 Kt—Q2, etc.
200. 1 Q—B6, Q—R7 ; 2 Q—QB3, Q—KB5 ; 3 Kt—KB6ch, QxKt ; 4 Q—QB4ch, etc.

4

CPSIA information can be obtained
at www.ICGtesting.com
Printed in the USA
LVHW081355130320
649991LV00013B/516